I thoug[ht] [you would]
enjoy this book.
We await in joyful
anticipation for the
arrival of _ _ _ _ _ _

Love & Thoughts
Paula   2/4/06

Kids Talk About Heaven

ALSO BY ERIC MARSHALL

Children's Letters to God
(with Stuart Hample)

Grandma, Grandpa and Me
(with Stuart Hample)

Kids Talk About Heaven

How You Get There, and How You Don't

Compiled by
Eric Marshall

ILLUSTRATED BY JENNIFER GOODSON

KYLE CATHIE LIMITED

Published in Great Britain in 2003 by
Kyle Cathie Limited
122 Arlington Road
London NW1 7HP
general.enquiries@kyle-cathie.com
www.kylecathie.com

First published in the USA by Crown Publishers, New York, New York
Member of the Crown Publishing Group, a division of Random House, Inc.

ISBN 1 85626 585 4

Design by Karen Minster

Eric Marshall is hereby identified as the author of this work in accordance
with Section 77 of the Copyright, Designs and Patents Act 1988.

A Cataloguing in Publication record for this title is available from the British
Library.

Printed and bound in Singapore by Star Standard

Contents

Introduction...7

HEAVEN...9
You just believe it

QUESTIONS, BIG AND SMALL...31
How good do you have to be?

THE OPPOSITE OF HEAVEN...47
Bad things

ANGELS, DEVILS, SAINTS, CELEBRITIES...63
You could get a lot of autographs

HEREAFTER...83
The forever part

Introduction

Is there really a Heaven? Where is it? Who gets to go there? If you don't get in, where do they send you? Does everyone get to be an angel? Can you meet anyone you want in Heaven? What happens if you don't believe in it? Is the Devil always waiting to get you?

Children are natural-born philosophers. They wonder and speculate and worry about a great many things – why the grass is green and the sky blue, how many flavours there are, what's right and what's wrong, where we come from and where we go. Their world is a vast arena of speculation and discovery. They pick up pieces of information, myths, beliefs and explanations, and decode and process them in their own special way. What results may sometimes appear strange but it is always heartfelt and honest, and often touching.

Their concerns resonate in our adult lives as well. They bring us back to a time when we knew much less and wondered much more, and when we allowed ourselves to think about the really important things without self-consciousness or inhibition. Children, of course, have little sense of their own mortality. Life is forever for them. But they are also intrigued by and often apprehensive about 'what happens next' and how it will all turn out.

What follows is a collection of children's questions, affirmations, doubts and speculations about what lies in store, the expression of their innermost thoughts and concerns. Naïve, simple, direct and honest, they are sometimes disarmingly wise and often full of optimism and humour. They provide a reassuring link for us as adults to join children in pondering the eternal questions.

Heaven

Celestial music is what
they have in Heaven and
in church. It's OK, but
not all the time.
            Caroline

Anybody can get into Heaven. You don't have to be important or famous or rich. You can even be dumb, but you have to be good, and that's up to you. Nicholas

If you believe in God
he'll take care of all the details.

— Winston —

If you're Christian you go to one part of Heaven and if you're Jewish you go to another. It's really the same place but I guess the food is different.

David

CAROLE

There are all kinds of
bad things you can't do
if you want to get ~~in~~ into
heaven. Sometimes you don't
even know that you're doing
them.

Only your soul goes
to Heaven There not
interested
in the rest of you. Chris

You can't get there unless you're dead
and even then it's hard to get in.
They ask you a lot of questions
at the gate but they already
know the answers so you better
tell the truth.

Walter

WHEN YOU GET TO
HEAVEN YOU HAVE A

LIFE OR BLISS.
I'M NOT SURE WHAT
BLISS IS BUT IT'S
GOT TO BE GOOD.
TONYA

Heaven is the place your spirit goes. Our Minister says that Heaven is inside us so you don't have to go far to get there.

Carmella

It's Just Goodness
And Happiness And Warm.

CAMERON

What you get in Heaven is Salvation. That's something you've got to Have

Brittany

Heaven is not a place. It's just an idea. But it's a very strong idea, because if we didn't have it we wouldn't have any hope.

Andy

Heaven is all the love in the world collected in one place.

I like the idea of
Heaven but I'm not
in any hurry to get there.

Julia

Questions, Big and Small

If you're only average good
Can you still get in?

JESS

Do kids get to stay with other kids or do they have to stay with grown-ups?

Jackson

I want to be invisible
and come back and see all
the people I know and
listen to what they
say and make them do things
I want them to do
and get even too.
I guess they don't want
you to do that though
do they?
<u>Shalequa</u>

Do you get to wear
different close or do you
have to go around in your
angl suit all the time?

Morgan

What if the Devil makes
you do something bad
even if you don't want to?
Will they hold that against
you? what if somebody tells
you it's all right and then
it turns out that it
isn't?

Kelly

My Grandma says the good die young.
I don't want to die young, so what
am I supposed to do.

by Mara

HOW HIGH UP IS IT
BECAUSE SOMETIMES

MY NOSE BLEEDS.

TIM

If you have to go to HeLL do
they Tell your parents?

Chris

If you don't believe
in Heaven or Hell
will they leave you
alone?

Jason

When you go to heaven
are you still
the same person
you were?
If you had a limp
do you still have one
in Heaven or
do you become new?

Cynthia

The Opposite of Heaven

Hell is a bad place,
worse than camp.

Brent

Hell is the opposite of Heaven. You always have to have opposites so you can tell how you're doing.

Orly

Are there different
places in Hell if
you were just bad
but not terrible?

Shana

YOU GO TO HELL
FOR SINNING.
A LOT OF STUFF
YOU LIKE TO DO
IS SINNING
SO YOU GOT TO BE
VERY CAREFUL,
BILL

It's always DARK
In hell. You
Never Know Who's
going to grab you or
What you will
step in.

andrew

They have something
called Hellfire
and Brimstone
and it happens
in the bottomless
pit. No thanks,
        —Samalia

I bet the Devil
would not let
a fireman come
there because
he would know how to
put out all the
fires,

Diana

They tell you all about Hell
so you will want to be good
and go to Heaven.

Tyler

God made both Heaven
and Hell so every-
body would have a
place to go.

Annie

You go up to heaven
and down to hell.
I like it here in the middle.

Erin

Angels, Devils, Saints, Celebrities

An angel comes and gets you and takes you to Heaven.

They're very nice and will even give you a drink when you get thirsty.

Betsy

The angels are like God's messengers in Heaven and they do special jobs for him. A guardian angel is someone who watches out for you. When you talk to them they hear you and they help you to see what's right and what's wrong.

Lesha

My Mom calls me a
little devil. She
means I got into
mischief. But I'm not a
real devil. He's a bad
person. She's just
joking.

Ashton K

There are a lot
of saints. There's
even a Saint Bernard.
It's a kind of dog.
Don't ask me how
that happened.

Frankie.

Some angels have rotten jobs like

the Angel of Death who tells
you your dead. The Angel of Mercy is
nicer. She can't stop you dying
but she can make it so it doesn't

hurt.   Yurie

Martyrs are people
who are so good that
somebody kills them.
They become angels
and they go right to
heaven.

Mary

St. Valentine is the
Saint of love
What a rotten
Job.
ZACH

I hear the devil
can make it so
that you always win
but then he's got
you in his Power.
You have to be
careful about outside
help. Carter

Martyrs go to Heaven
because they suffer
a lot here.
If you're very unhappy on
earth then they will try
to make it up to you.

Arlene

Satan is another name for the Devil. He has lots of names and they're all scary. Mostly he has horns and smells bad, but when he dresses up he looks very cool and can make you do bad things.
                    —Keaton

you cant blame
the devil. Hes
just doing his job.
Beth

I want to get to meet
Abraham Lincoln but
not if he is so old that he
has lost his mind and
can't even talk like my
great grandmother.

Miles

Lots of famous people
are in HEAVEN. You
could get alot of
autographs.
ALEX

Hereafter

What scares me is the
   for ever
   part.
I wish they would make
life longer and Heaven shorter.

PAUL

If you never get born you never have to die, but you miss a lot.

Alison

You have an eternal soul
so you GOT To Take Care oF iT
wheN you're alive.
It lasTs a lot loNGer ThaN you do.

Willy

Maybe you just become music and float in the air and when someone hears you they say "Listen to that Heavenly music".

Peter

Where you go is called the hereafter, but it's not here and it happens after.

Benji

Some people believe you
come back from heaven as
something else. Some people
believe anything. Ted

I think it's like a feeling.
It's not like a place
with streets and houses
but it's just somewhere
you want to stay forever.
It's like a nice dream.

Sharon

I think you become a little
light like a candle and nothing
can blow you out.

Lisa